Organize Your Life.

THIS BOOK BELONGS TO:

CONTACT INFO:

Disclaimer and Warning:

ISBN: 1441496750

EAN 13: 9781441496751

Printed in the USA

Internet Password Vault

An Alphabetical Listing of Your Logins and Passwords

SOUL SALON INTERNATIONAL

_A_

Website_____
Login_____
Password_____

Website_____
Login_____
Password_____

Website_____
Login_____
Password_____

Website_____
Login_____
Password_____

Website_____
Login_____
Password_____

Website_____
Login_____
Password_____

Website_____
Login_____
Password_____

Website_____
Login_____
Password_____

_A_

Website_____
Login_____
Password_____

Website_____
Login_____
Password_____

Website_____
Login_____
Password_____

Website_____
Login_____
Password_____

Website_____
Login_____
Password_____

Website_____
Login_____
Password_____

Website_____
Login_____
Password_____

Website_____
Login_____
Password_____

B

Website_____
Login_____
Password_____

Website_____
Login_____
Password_____

Website_____
Login_____
Password_____

Website_____
Login_____
Password_____

Website_____
Login_____
Password_____

Website_____
Login_____
Password_____

Website_____
Login_____
Password_____

Website_____
Login_____
Password_____

B

Website_____
Login_____
Password_____

Website_____
Login_____
Password_____

Website_____
Login_____
Password_____

Website_____
Login_____
Password_____

Website_____
Login_____
Password_____

Website_____
Login_____
Password_____

Website_____
Login_____
Password_____

Website_____
Login_____
Password_____

C

Website_____
Login_____
Password_____

Website_____
Login_____
Password_____

Website_____
Login_____
Password_____

Website_____
Login_____
Password_____

Website_____
Login_____
Password_____

Website_____
Login_____
Password_____

Website_____
Login_____
Password_____

Website_____
Login_____
Password_____

C

Website_____
Login_____
Password_____

Website_____
Login_____
Password_____

Website_____
Login_____
Password_____

Website_____
Login_____
Password_____

Website_____
Login_____
Password_____

Website_____
Login_____
Password_____

Website_____
Login_____
Password_____

Website_____
Login_____
Password_____

D

Website_____
Login_____
Password_____

Website_____
Login_____
Password_____

Website_____
Login_____
Password_____

Website_____
Login_____
Password_____

Website_____
Login_____
Password_____

Website_____
Login_____
Password_____

Website_____
Login_____
Password_____

Website_____
Login_____
Password_____

D

Website_____
Login_____
Password_____

Website_____
Login_____
Password_____

Website_____
Login_____
Password_____

Website_____
Login_____
Password_____

Website_____
Login_____
Password_____

Website_____
Login_____
Password_____

Website_____
Login_____
Password_____

Website_____
Login_____
Password_____

_E_

Website_____
Login_____
Password_____

Website_____
Login_____
Password_____

Website_____
Login_____
Password_____

Website_____
Login_____
Password_____

Website_____
Login_____
Password_____

Website_____
Login_____
Password_____

Website_____
Login_____
Password_____

Website_____
Login_____
Password_____

E

Website_____
Login_____
Password_____

Website_____
Login_____
Password_____

Website_____
Login_____
Password_____

Website_____
Login_____
Password_____

Website_____
Login_____
Password_____

Website_____
Login_____
Password_____

Website_____
Login_____
Password_____

Website_____
Login_____
Password_____

_F_

Website_____
Login_____
Password_____

Website_____
Login_____
Password_____

Website_____
Login_____
Password_____

Website_____
Login_____
Password_____

Website_____
Login_____
Password_____

Website_____
Login_____
Password_____

Website_____
Login_____
Password_____

Website_____
Login_____
Password_____

F

Website_____
Login_____
Password_____

Website_____
Login_____
Password_____

Website_____
Login_____
Password_____

Website_____
Login_____
Password_____

Website_____
Login_____
Password_____

Website_____
Login_____
Password_____

Website_____
Login_____
Password_____

Website_____
Login_____
Password_____

G

Website_____
Login_____
Password_____

Website_____
Login_____
Password_____

Website_____
Login_____
Password_____

Website_____
Login_____
Password_____

Website_____
Login_____
Password_____

Website_____
Login_____
Password_____

Website_____
Login_____
Password_____

Website_____
Login_____
Password_____

G

Website_____
Login_____
Password_____

Website_____
Login_____
Password_____

Website_____
Login_____
Password_____

Website_____
Login_____
Password_____

Website_____
Login_____
Password_____

Website_____
Login_____
Password_____

Website_____
Login_____
Password_____

Website_____
Login_____
Password_____

$\mathcal{H}$

Website_____
Login_____
Password_____

Website_____
Login_____
Password_____

Website_____
Login_____
Password_____

Website_____
Login_____
Password_____

Website_____
Login_____
Password_____

Website_____
Login_____
Password_____

Website_____
Login_____
Password_____

Website_____
Login_____
Password_____

H

Website_____
Login_____
Password_____

Website_____
Login_____
Password_____

Website_____
Login_____
Password_____

Website_____
Login_____
Password_____

Website_____
Login_____
Password_____

Website_____
Login_____
Password_____

Website_____
Login_____
Password_____

Website_____
Login_____
Password_____

I

Website_____
Login_____
Password_____

Website_____
Login_____
Password_____

Website_____
Login_____
Password_____

Website_____
Login_____
Password_____

Website_____
Login_____
Password_____

Website_____
Login_____
Password_____

Website_____
Login_____
Password_____

Website_____
Login_____
Password_____

J

Website_____
Login_____
Password_____

Website_____
Login_____
Password_____

Website_____
Login_____
Password_____

Website_____
Login_____
Password_____

Website_____
Login_____
Password_____

Website_____
Login_____
Password_____

Website_____
Login_____
Password_____

Website_____
Login_____
Password_____

J

Website_____
Login_____
Password_____

Website_____
Login_____
Password_____

Website_____
Login_____
Password_____

Website_____
Login_____
Password_____

Website_____
Login_____
Password_____

Website_____
Login_____
Password_____

Website_____
Login_____
Password_____

Website_____
Login_____
Password_____

J

Website_____
Login_____
Password_____

Website_____
Login_____
Password_____

Website_____
Login_____
Password_____

Website_____
Login_____
Password_____

Website_____
Login_____
Password_____

Website_____
Login_____
Password_____

Website_____
Login_____
Password_____

Website_____
Login_____
Password_____

K

Website_____
Login_____
Password_____

Website_____
Login_____
Password_____

Website_____
Login_____
Password_____

Website_____
Login_____
Password_____

Website_____
Login_____
Password_____

Website_____
Login_____
Password_____

Website_____
Login_____
Password_____

Website_____
Login_____
Password_____

K

Website_____
Login_____
Password_____

Website_____
Login_____
Password_____

Website_____
Login_____
Password_____

Website_____
Login_____
Password_____

Website_____
Login_____
Password_____

Website_____
Login_____
Password_____

Website_____
Login_____
Password_____

Website_____
Login_____
Password_____

L

Website_____
Login_____
Password_____

Website_____
Login_____
Password_____

Website_____
Login_____
Password_____

Website_____
Login_____
Password_____

Website_____
Login_____
Password_____

Website_____
Login_____
Password_____

Website_____
Login_____
Password_____

Website_____
Login_____
Password_____

L

Website_____
Login_____
Password_____

Website_____
Login_____
Password_____

Website_____
Login_____
Password_____

Website_____
Login_____
Password_____

Website_____
Login_____
Password_____

Website_____
Login_____
Password_____

Website_____
Login_____
Password_____

Website_____
Login_____
Password_____

M

Website_____
Login_____
Password_____

Website_____
Login_____
Password_____

Website_____
Login_____
Password_____

Website_____
Login_____
Password_____

Website_____
Login_____
Password_____

Website_____
Login_____
Password_____

Website_____
Login_____
Password_____

Website_____
Login_____
Password_____

M

Website_____
Login_____
Password_____

Website_____
Login_____
Password_____

Website_____
Login_____
Password_____

Website_____
Login_____
Password_____

Website_____
Login_____
Password_____

Website_____
Login_____
Password_____

Website_____
Login_____
Password_____

Website_____
Login_____
Password_____

Website_____
Login_____
Password_____

Website_____
Login_____
Password_____

Website_____
Login_____
Password_____

Website_____
Login_____
Password_____

Website_____
Login_____
Password_____

Website_____
Login_____
Password_____

Website_____
Login_____
Password_____

Website_____
Login_____
Password_____

Website_____
Login_____
Password_____

N

Website_____
Login_____
Password_____

Website_____
Login_____
Password_____

Website_____
Login_____
Password_____

Website_____
Login_____
Password_____

Website_____
Login_____
Password_____

Website_____
Login_____
Password_____

Website_____
Login_____
Password_____

Website_____
Login_____
Password_____

O

Website_____
Login_____
Password_____

Website_____
Login_____
Password_____

Website_____
Login_____
Password_____

Website_____
Login_____
Password_____

Website_____
Login_____
Password_____

Website_____
Login_____
Password_____

Website_____
Login_____
Password_____

Website_____
Login_____
Password_____

O

Website_____
Login_____
Password_____

Website_____
Login_____
Password_____

Website_____
Login_____
Password_____

Website_____
Login_____
Password_____

Website_____
Login_____
Password_____

Website_____
Login_____
Password_____

Website_____
Login_____
Password_____

Website_____
Login_____
Password_____

P

Website_____
Login_____
Password_____

Website_____
Login_____
Password_____

Website_____
Login_____
Password_____

Website_____
Login_____
Password_____

Website_____
Login_____
Password_____

Website_____
Login_____
Password_____

Website_____
Login_____
Password_____

Website_____
Login_____
Password_____

P

Website_____
Login_____
Password_____

Website_____
Login_____
Password_____

Website_____
Login_____
Password_____

Website_____
Login_____
Password_____

Website_____
Login_____
Password_____

Website_____
Login_____
Password_____

Website_____
Login_____
Password_____

Website_____
Login_____
Password_____

Q

Website_____

Login_____

Password_____

Website_____

Login_____

Password_____

Website_____

Login_____

Password_____

Website_____

Login_____

Password_____

Website_____

Login_____

Password_____

Website_____

Login_____

Password_____

Website_____

Login_____

Password_____

Website_____

Login_____

Password_____

Q

Website_____

Login_____

Password_____

Website_____

Login_____

Password_____

Website_____

Login_____

Password_____

Website_____

Login_____

Password_____

Website_____

Login_____

Password_____

Website_____

Login_____

Password_____

Website_____

Login_____

Password_____

Website_____

Login_____

Password_____

$\mathcal{R}$

Website_____
Login_____
Password_____

Website_____
Login_____
Password_____

Website_____
Login_____
Password_____

Website_____
Login_____
Password_____

Website_____
Login_____
Password_____

Website_____
Login_____
Password_____

Website_____
Login_____
Password_____

Website_____
Login_____
Password_____

$\mathcal{R}$

Website_____
Login_____
Password_____

Website_____
Login_____
Password_____

Website_____
Login_____
Password_____

Website_____
Login_____
Password_____

Website_____
Login_____
Password_____

Website_____
Login_____
Password_____

Website_____
Login_____
Password_____

Website_____
Login_____
Password_____

S

Website_____
Login_____
Password_____

Website_____
Login_____
Password_____

Website_____
Login_____
Password_____

Website_____
Login_____
Password_____

Website_____
Login_____
Password_____

Website_____
Login_____
Password_____

Website_____
Login_____
Password_____

Website_____
Login_____
Password_____

S

Website_____
Login_____
Password_____

Website_____
Login_____
Password_____

Website_____
Login_____
Password_____

Website_____
Login_____
Password_____

Website_____
Login_____
Password_____

Website_____
Login_____
Password_____

Website_____
Login_____
Password_____

Website_____
Login_____
Password_____

Website_____
Login_____
Password_____

T

Website_____
Login_____
Password_____

Website_____
Login_____
Password_____

Website_____
Login_____
Password_____

Website_____
Login_____
Password_____

Website_____
Login_____
Password_____

Website_____
Login_____
Password_____

Website_____
Login_____
Password_____

Website_____
Login_____
Password_____

T

Website_____
Login_____
Password_____

Website_____
Login_____
Password_____

Website_____
Login_____
Password_____

Website_____
Login_____
Password_____

Website_____
Login_____
Password_____

Website_____
Login_____
Password_____

Website_____
Login_____
Password_____

Website_____
Login_____
Password_____

$\mathcal{U}$

Website_____
Login_____
Password_____

Website_____
Login_____
Password_____

Website_____
Login_____
Password_____

Website_____
Login_____
Password_____

Website_____
Login_____
Password_____

Website_____
Login_____
Password_____

Website_____
Login_____
Password_____

Website_____
Login_____
Password_____

U

Website_____
Login_____
Password_____

Website_____
Login_____
Password_____

Website_____
Login_____
Password_____

Website_____
Login_____
Password_____

Website_____
Login_____
Password_____

Website_____
Login_____
Password_____

Website_____
Login_____
Password_____

Website_____
Login_____
Password_____

V

Website_____

Login_____

Password_____

Website_____

Login_____

Password_____

Website_____

Login_____

Password_____

Website_____

Login_____

Password_____

Website_____

Login_____

Password_____

Website_____

Login_____

Password_____

Website_____

Login_____

Password_____

Website_____

Login_____

Password_____

V

Website_____
Login_____
Password_____

Website_____
Login_____
Password_____

Website_____
Login_____
Password_____

Website_____
Login_____
Password_____

Website_____
Login_____
Password_____

Website_____
Login_____
Password_____

Website_____
Login_____
Password_____

Website_____
Login_____
Password_____

W

Website_____
Login_____
Password_____

Website_____
Login_____
Password_____

Website_____
Login_____
Password_____

Website_____
Login_____
Password_____

Website_____
Login_____
Password_____

Website_____
Login_____
Password_____

Website_____
Login_____
Password_____

Website_____
Login_____
Password_____

W

Website_____
Login_____
Password_____

Website_____
Login_____
Password_____

Website_____
Login_____
Password_____

Website_____
Login_____
Password_____

Website_____
Login_____
Password_____

Website_____
Login_____
Password_____

Website_____
Login_____
Password_____

Website_____
Login_____
Password_____

$\mathcal{X}$

Website_____
Login_____
Password_____

Website_____
Login_____
Password_____

Website_____
Login_____
Password_____

Website_____
Login_____
Password_____

Website_____
Login_____
Password_____

Website_____
Login_____
Password_____

Website_____
Login_____
Password_____

Website_____
Login_____
Password_____

χ

Website_____
Login_____
Password_____

Website_____
Login_____
Password_____

Website_____
Login_____
Password_____

Website_____
Login_____
Password_____

Website_____
Login_____
Password_____

Website_____
Login_____
Password_____

Website_____
Login_____
Password_____

Website_____
Login_____
Password_____

Website_____
Login_____
Password_____

Website_____
Login_____
Password_____

Website_____
Login_____
Password_____

Website_____
Login_____
Password_____

Website_____
Login_____
Password_____

Website_____
Login_____
Password_____

Website_____
Login_____
Password_____

Website_____
Login_____
Password_____

Website_____
Login_____
Password_____

γ

Website_____

Login_____

Password_____

Website_____

Login_____

Password_____

Website_____

Login_____

Password_____

Website_____

Login_____

Password_____

Website_____

Login_____

Password_____

Website_____

Login_____

Password_____

Website_____

Login_____

Password_____

Website_____

Login_____

Password_____

Z

Website_____

Login_____

Password_____

Website_____

Login_____

Password_____

Website_____

Login_____

Password_____

Website_____

Login_____

Password_____

Website_____

Login_____

Password_____

Website_____

Login_____

Password_____

Website_____

Login_____

Password_____

Website_____

Login_____

Password_____

Z

Website_____
Login_____
Password_____

Website_____
Login_____
Password_____

Website_____
Login_____
Password_____

Website_____
Login_____
Password_____

Website_____
Login_____
Password_____

Website_____
Login_____
Password_____

Website_____
Login_____
Password_____

Website_____
Login_____
Password_____